S0-AKE-593

KEEPSAKES

TRUTH &
BEAUTY

All rights reserved: no part of this publication
may be reproduced, stored in a retrieval system, or transmitted
in any form or by any means, electronic, mechanical,
photocopying or otherwise, without the prior
written permission of the Publishers.

First published in the United States by
Salem House Publishers, 1989, 462 Boston Street,
Topsfield, Massachusetts, 01983.

Copyright © Swallow Publishing Ltd 1989

Conceived and produced by
Swallow Books, 260 Pentonville Road,
London N1 9JY

ISBN: 0 88162 381 4
Art Director: Elaine Partington
Editor: Catherine Tilley
Designer: Jean Hoyes
Picture Researcher: Liz Eddison
Printed in Hong Kong by Imago Publishing Limited

KEEPSAKES

TRUTH & BEAUTY

Compiled by
Samantha Younger

Salem House

She Walks in Beauty

She walks in beauty, like the night
   Of cloudless climes and starry skies;
And all that's best of dark and bright
   Meet in her aspect and her eyes:
Thus mellowed to that tender light
   Which heaven to gaudy day denies.

One shade the more, one ray the less,
   Had half impaired the nameless grace
Which waves in every raven tress,
   Or softly lightens o'er her face;
Where thoughts serenely sweet express
   How pure, how dear their dwelling place.

And on that cheek, and o'er that brow,
   So soft, so calm, yet eloquent,
The smiles that win, the tints that glow,
   But tell of days in goodness spent,
A mind at peace with all below,
   A heart whose love is innocent!

LORD BYRON

Alone with the Earth

MOVING UP THE sweet short turf, at every step my heart seemed to obtain a wider horizon of feeling; with every inhalation of rich pure air, a deeper desire.... By the time I had reached the summit I had entirely forgotten the petty circumstances and the annoyances of existence. I felt myself, myself.... I was utterly alone with the sun and the earth. Lying down on the grass, I spoke in my soul to the earth, the sun, the air, and the distant sea far beyond sight. I thought of the earth's firmness – I felt it bear me up; through the grassy couch there came an influence as if I could feel the great earth speaking to me. I thought of the wandering air – it's pureness, which is its beauty; the air touched me and gave me something of itself. I spoke to the sea: though so far, in my mind I saw it, green at the rim of the earth and blue in deeper ocean; I desired to have its strength, its mystery and glory. Then I addressed the sun, desiring the soul equivalent of his light and brilliance, his endurance and unwearied race. I turned to the blue heaven over, gazing into its depth, inhaling its exquisite colour and sweetness. The rich blue of the unattainable flower of the sky drew my soul towards it, and there it rested, for pure colour is rest of heart.

RICHARD JEFFERIES

The Importance of Being Truthful

Algernon: Why are you Ernest in town and Jack in the country?

Jack: My dear Algy, I don't know whether you will be able to understand my real motives. You are hardly serious enough. When one is placed in the position of guardian, one has to adopt a very high moral tone on all subjects. It's one's duty to do so. And as a high moral tone can hardly be said to conduce very much to either one's health or one's happiness, in order to get up to town I have always pretended to have a younger brother of the name of Ernest, who lives in the Albany, and gets into the most dreadful scrapes. That, may dear Algy, is the whole truth pure and simple.

Algernon: The truth is rarely pure and never simple. Modern life would be very tedious if it were either, and modern literature a complete impossibility!

Jack: That wouldn't be at all a bad thing.

Algernon: Literary criticism is not your forte, my dear fellow.... You should leave that to people who haven't been at a University. They do it so well in the daily papers.

OSCAR WILDE

The Daffodils

I wandered lonely as a cloud
    That floats on high o'er vales and hills,
When all at once I saw a crowd,
    A host, of golden daffodils;
Beside the lake, beneath the trees,
    Fluttering and dancing in the breeze.

The waves beside them danced; but they
    Out-did the sparkling weaves in glee:
A poet could not but be gay,
    In such a jocund company:
I gazed – and gazed – but little thought
    What wealth the show to me had brought:

For oft, when on my couch I lie
    In vacant or in pensive mood,
They flash upon that inward eye
    Which is the bliss of solitude;
And then my heart with pleasure fills,
    And dances with the daffodils.

WILLIAM WORDSWORTH

Buddhist Wisdom

Look upon the world as you would on a bubble; look upon it as you would on a mirage; the king of death does not see him who thus looks down upon the world.

Come, look at this world, glittering like a royal chariot. The foolish are immersed in it, but the wise does not touch it.

Difficult it is to obtain birth as a human being; difficult is the life of mortals; difficult is the hearing of the True Law; difficult is the birth of the Awakened (the attainment of Buddhahood).

Health is the greatest of acquisitions; contentment the best riches; trust is the best of relationships; Nirvana the highest happiness.

Ahinsa (non-killing or non-injury), Truth, Non-stealing, Brahmacharya or Celibacy and Non-acceptance or renunciation – these are the five Yamas or precepts.

Speak the truth, do not yield to anger; give even though it be but little, to him who begs. By these three steps thou wilt go near the Gods.

SAYINGS OF THE BUDDHA

A Natural Virtue

LIFE APPEARS TO ME to be too short to be spent in nursing animosity, or registering wrongs. We are, and must be, one and all, burdened with faults in this world; but the time will soon come when, I trust, we shall put them off in putting off our corruptible bodies; when debasement and sin will fall from us with this cumbrous frame of flesh, and only the spark of the spirit will remain – the impalpable principle of life and thought, pure as when it left the Creator to inspire the creature; whence it came it will return, perhaps again to be communicated to some being higher than man.... Surely it will never, on the contrary, be suffered to degenerate from man to fiend? No; I cannot believe that; I hold another creed, which no one ever taught me, and which I seldom mention; but in which I delight, and to which I cling, for it extends hope to all; it makes Eternity a rest – a mighty home, not a terror and an abyss. Besides, with this creed, I can so clearly distinguish between the criminal and his crime; I can so sincerely forgive the first while I abhor the last: with this creed, revenge never worries my heart, degradation never too deeply disgusts me, injustice never crushes me too low; I live in calm, looking to the end.

CHARLOTTE BRONTE

Ode on a Grecian Urn

Thou still unravish'd bride of quietness,
   Thou foster-child of silence and slow time,
Sylvan historian, who canst thus express
   A flowery tale more sweetly than our rhyme:
What leaf-fring'd legend haunts about thy shape
   Of deities or mortals, or of both,
      In Tempe or the dales of Arcady?
What men or gods are these? What maidens loth?
   What mad pursuit? What struggle to escape?
      What pipes and timbrels? What wild ecstasy?

O Attic shape! Fair attitude! with brede
   Of marble men and maidens overwrought,
With forest branches and the trodden weed;
   Thou, silent form, dost tease us out of thought
As doth eternity: Cold Pastoral!
   When old age shall this generation waste,
      Thou shalt remain, in midst of other woe
Than ours, a friend to man, to whom thou say'st,
   'Beauty is truth, truth beauty,' – that is all
      Ye know on earth, and all ye need to know.

JOHN KEATS

Saying the Thing
Which Is Not

M Y MASTER heard me with great Appearances of Uneasiness in his Countenance; because *Doubting* or *not believing* are so little known in this Country that the Inhabitants cannot tell how to behave themselves under such Circumstances. And I remember in frequent Discourses with my Master concerning the Nature of Manhood, in other Parts of the World; having Occasion to talk of *Lying*, and *false Representation*, it was with much Difficulty that he comprehended what I meant; although he had otherwise a most acute Judgment. For he argued thus; That the Use of Speech was to make us understand one another, and to receive Information of Facts; now if any one *said the Thing which was not*, these Ends were defeated; because I cannot properly be said to understand him; and I am so far from receiving Information, that he leaves me worse than in Ignorance; for I am led to believe a Thing *Black* when it is *White* and *Short* when it is *Long*. And these were all the Notions he had concerning that Faculty of *Lying*, so perfectly well understood, and so universally practised among human Creatures.

JONATHAN SWIFT

To Helen

Helen, thy beauty is to me
   Like those Nicean barks of yore,
That gently, o'er a perfumed sea,
   The weary, wayworn wanderer bore
   To his own native shore.

On desperate seas long wont to roam,
   Thy hyacinth hair, thy classic face,
Thy Naiad airs have brought me home
   To the glory that was Greece,
   To the grandeur that was Rome.

Lo! in yon brilliant window niche,
   How statue-like I see thee stand,
   The agate lamp within thy hand!
Ah, Psyche, from the regions which
   Are Holy Land!

EDGAR ALLAN POE

Behind the Shadow

HE GLOOM OF THE WORLD is but a shadow. Behind it, yet within our reach, is joy. There is radiance and glory in the darkness, could we but see, and to see, we have only to look.

Life is so generous a giver but we, judging its gifts by their covering, cast them away as ugly or heavy or hard. Remove the covering, and you will find beneath it a living splendour, woven of love, by wisdom, with power: Welcome it, grasp it, and you touch the Angel's hand that brings it to you. Everything we call a trial, a sorrow, or a duty: believe me, that angel's hand is there, the gift is there, and the wonder of an over-shadowing Presence. Our joys, too: be not content with them as joys, they too conceal diviner gifts. Life is so full of meaning and of purpose, so full of beauty – beneath its covering – that you will find that earth but cloaks your heaven. Courage, then to claim it: that is all! But courage you have: and the knowledge that we are pilgrims together, wending through unknown country, home.

FRA GIOVANNI

An Afternoon Scene

F EBRUARY 22. Last night and today rainy and thick, till mid-afternoon, when the wind chopp'd round, the clouds swiftly drew off like curtains, the clear appear'd, and with it the fairest, grandest, most wondrous rainbow I ever saw, all complete, very vivid at its earth-ends, spreading vast effusions of illuminated haze, violet, yellow, drab-green in all directions overhead, through which the sun beam'd an indescribable utterance of color and light, so gorgeous yet so soft, such as I had never witness'd before. Then its continuance: a full hour pass'd before the last of those earth-ends disappear'd. The sky behind was all spread in translucent blue, with many little white clouds and edges. To these a sunset, filling, dominating the esthetic and soul senses, sumptuously, tenderly, full. I end this note by the pond, just light enough to see, through the evening shadows, the western reflections in its water-mirror surface, with inverted figures of trees. I hear now and then the *flup* of a pike leaping out, and rippling the water.

WALT WHITMAN

Advice for Life

Polonius. Give thy thoughts no tongue,
Nor any unproportion'd thought his act.
Be thou familiar, but by no means vulgar;
The friends thou hast, and their adoption tried,
Grapple them to thy soul with hoops of steel;
But do not dull thy palm with entertainment
Of each new-hatch'd, unfledg'd comrade. Beware
Of entrance to a quarrel, but, being in,
Bear't that th' opposed may beware of thee.
Give every man thine ear, but few thy voice;
Take each man's censure, but reserve thy judgment.
Costly thy habit as thy purse can buy,
But not express'd in fancy; rich, not gaudy;
For the apparel oft proclaims the man,
And they in France of the best rank and station
Are most select and generous, chief in that.
Neither a borrower, nor a lender be;
For loan oft loses both itself and friend,
And borrowing dulls the edge of husbandry.
This above all: to thine own self be true,
And it must follow, as the night the day,
Thou canst not then be false to any man.

WILLIAM SHAKESPEARE

How to Milk the Truth

THURSDAY, 21 JULY 1763. *Johnson*. 'We can have no dependence upon that instinctive, that constitutional goodness which is not founded upon principle. I grant you that such a man may be a very amiable member of society. I can conceive him placed in such a situation that he is not much tempted to deviate from what is right; and as every man prefers virtue, when there is not some strong incitement to transgress its precepts, I can conceive him doing nothing wrong. But if such a man stood in need of money, I should not like to trust him; and I should certainly not trust him with young ladies, for *there* there is always temptation. Hume, and other sceptical innovators, are vain men, and will gratify themselves at any expense. Truth will not afford sufficient food to their vanity; so they have betaken themselves to error. Truth, Sir, is a cow which will yield such people no more milk, and so they are gone to milk the bull. If I could have allowed myself to gratify my vanity at the expense of truth, what fame might I have acquired.'

JAMES BOSWELL

Rowlandson Delin 1819

Out of Time

A thing of beauty is a joy for ever:
Its loveliness increases; it will never
Pass into nothingness; but still will keep
A bower quiet for us, and a sleep
Full of sweet dreams, and health, and quiet breathing.

JOHN KEATS

When forty winters shall besiege thy brow,
And dig deep trenches in thy beauty's field,
Thy youth's proud livery, so gaz'd on now,
Will be a tatter'd weed, of small worth held:
Then being ask'd where all thy beauty lies,
Where all the treasure of thy lusty days,
To say, within thine own deep-sunken eyes,
Were an all-eating shame and thriftless praise.
How much more praise deserv'd thy beauty's use,
If thou couldst answer, 'This fair child of mine
Shall sum my count, and make my old excuse,'
Proving his beauty by succession thine!
    This were to be new made when thou art old,
    And see thy blood warm when thou feel'st it
    cold.

WILLIAM SHAKESPEARE

The Sovereign Good

RUTH, WHICH ONLY doth judge itself, teacheth, that the inquiry of truth, which is the love-making, or wooing of it, the knowledge of truth, which is the presence of it, and the belief of truth, which is the enjoying of it, is the sovereign good of human nature. The first creature of God, in the works of the days, was the light of the sense: the last was the light of reason: and his sabbath work ever since, is the illumination of his Spirit. First, he breathed light upon the face of the matter, or chaos; then he breathed light into the face of man; and still he breathed and inspireth light into the face of his chosen.... Certainly, it is heaven upon earth to have a man's mind move in charity, rest in providence, and turn upon the poles of truth.

FRANCIS BACON

When all is done and said, in the end thus shall you find,
  He most of all doth bathe in bliss that hath a quiet mind.
And, clear from worldly cares, to deem can be content
  The sweetest time in all his life in thinking to be spent.

THOMAS, LORD VAUX

Beautiful Nairn

All ye tourists who wish to be away
    From the crowded city for a brief holiday;
The town of Nairn is worth a visit, I do confess,
    And it's only about fifteen miles from Inverness.

And in the summer season it's a very popular bathing-place,
    And the visitors from London and Edinburgh finds solace,
As they walk along the yellow sand beach inhaling fresh air;
    Besides, there's every accommodation for ladies and
        gentlemen there.

Then there's a large number of bathing coaches there,
    And the climate is salubrious, and very warm the air;
And every convenience is within the bathers' reach,
    Besides, there's very beautiful walks by the sea beach.

The visitors to Nairn can pass away the time agreeably,
    By viewing Tarbetness, which slopes downwards to the sea;
And Queen Street is one of the prettiest thoroughfares,
    Because there's splendid shops in it, and stocked with
        different wares.

WILLIAM McGONAGALL

To a Child Five Years Old

Fairest flower, all flowers excelling,
    Which in Eden's garden grew;
Flowers of Eve's embowered dwelling
    Are, my fair one, types of you.
Mark, my Polly, how the roses
    Emulate thy damask cheek;
How the bud its sweets discloses –
    Buds thy opening bloom bespeak.
Lilies are, by plain direction,
    Emblems of a double kind;
Emblems of thy fair complexion,
    Emblems of thy fairer mind.
But, dear girl, both flowers and beauty
    Blossom, fade, and die away;
Then pursue good sense and duty,
    Evergreens that ne'er decay.

NATHANIEL COTTON

The Flowering of Virtue

LET US APPROACH and admire Beauty, whose revelation to man we now celebrate – Beauty, welcome as the sun wherever it pleases to shine, which pleases everybody with it and with themselves. Wonderful is its charm. It seems sufficient to itself. The lover cannot paint his maiden to his fancy poor and solitary. Like a tree in flower, so much soft, budding, informing loveliness is society for itself; and she teaches his eye why Beauty was ever painted with Loves and Graces attending her steps. Her existence makes the world rich.... His friends find in her a likeness to her mother, or her sister, or to persons not of her blood. The lover sees no resemblance except to summer evenings and diamond mornings, to rainbows and the song of birds. Beauty is ever that divine thing the ancients esteemed it. It is, they said, the flowering of virtue. Who can analyze the nameless charm which glances from one and another face and form? We are touched with emotions of tenderness and complacency, but we cannot find whereat this dainty emotion, this wandering gleam, point. It is destroyed for the imagination by any attempt to refer it to organization.

RALPH WALDO EMERSON

A Blessed Woman

HO CAN FIND a virtuous woman? Her price is far above rubies. The heart of her husband doth safely trust in her, so that he shall have no need of spoil. She will do him good and not evil all the days of her life. She seeketh wool and flax, and worketh willingly with her hands. She is like the merchant's ships: she bringeth her food from afar. She perceiveth that her merchandise is good; her candle goeth not out by night. She layeth her hands to the spindle, and her hands hold the distaff. She stretcheth out her hand to the poor; yea, she reacheth forth her hands to the needy. She is not afraid of the snow for her household, for all her household are clothed with scarlet. She maketh herself coverings of tapestry; her clothing is silk and purple. She maketh fine linen, and selleth it; and delivereth girdles unto the merchant. Strength and honour are her clothing, and she shall rejoice in time to come. She opened her mouth with wisdom, and in her tongue is the law of kindness. She looketh well to the ways of her household, and eateth not the bread of idleness. Her children arise up and call her blessed; her husband also, and he praiseth her.

SOLOMON

The Universal Hymn

The spacious firmament on high,
   With all the blue ethereal sky,
And spangled heavens, a shining frame,
   Their great Original proclaim.
Th' unwearied Sun from day to day
   Does his Creator's power display;
And publishes to every land
   The work of an Almighty hand.

Soon as the evening shades prevail.
   The Moon takes up the wondrous tale;
And nightly to the listening Earth
   Repeats the story of her birth
Whilst all the stars that round her burn,
   And all the planets in their turn,
Confirm the tidings as they roll,
   And spread the truth from pole to pole.

... In Reason's ear they all rejoice,
   And utter forth a glorious voice;
For ever singing as they shine,
   'The Hand that made us is divine.'

JOSEPH ADDISON

Sources and Acknowledgments

For permission to reproduce illustrations, the publishers thank the following: Bridgeman Art Library, Sam Elder, Mary Evans Picture Library, E. T. Archive, the Mansell Collection and Spink & Son Ltd.